SPORTS ZONE

GIRLS' LACROSSE

A Guide for Players and Fans

BY HEATHER WILLIAMS

CAPSTONE PRESS
a capstone imprint

Fact Finders Books are published by Capstone
1710 Roe Crest Drive, North Mankato, Minnesota 56003
www.capstonepub.com

Editorial Credits
Lauren Dupuis-Perez, editor; Sara Radka, designer;
Eric Gohl, media researcher; Laura Manthe, production specialist

Photo Credits
Getty Images: beardean, 28, Bill Truslow, 29, Comstock, 11 (top), iacona,
cover (background), 10-11, kschultze, 8-9, Michael Steele, 4, Michael
Steele, 14, Michael Steele, 17, Michael Steele, 25, nycshooter, 27, Omar
Rawlings, cover (foreground), 23; Newscom: Icon Sportswire/Andy
Mead, 22, Icon Sportswire/YCJ/Andy Mead, 19, Icon Sportswire/
YCJ/Andy Mead, 20, ZUMA Press/Cal Sport Media/John Mersits, 24;
Pixabay: InTune, 9 (front), background; Shutterstock: CatwalkPhotos, 10
(bottom), James A Boardman, 18, Peter Dean, 12; Wikimedia: Gift of Mrs.
Joseph Harrison, Jr., 7, Smithsonian American Art Museum, 6

Library of Congress Cataloging-in-Publication Data
Names: Williams, Heather, 1974- author.
Title: Girls' lacrosse: a guide for players and fans / by Heather Williams.
Description: North Mankato, Minnesota: Capstone Press, [2019] |
Series: Fact finders. sports zone | Audience: Ages: 8-9. |
Audience: Grades: K-3.
Identifiers: LCCN 2019005980| ISBN 9781543574272 (hardcover) | ISBN
    9781543574609 (pbk.) | ISBN 9781543574289 (ebook pdf)
Subjects: LCSH: Lacrosse for girls—Juvenile literature.
Classification: LCC GV989.15 .W55 2019 | DDC 796.36/2082—dc23
LC record available at https://lccn.loc.gov/2019005980

All internet sites in the back matter were available and accurate when
this book was sent to press.

TABLE OF CONTENTS

Introduction...4

Lacrosse History...6

Gear of the Game.......................................10

Lacrosse Rules..14

Strategies to Succeed..............................20

Ready to Play?...26

Glossary 30

Read More..31

Internet Sites..31

Index 32

INTRODUCTION

In 2017 Taylor Cummings played in her first US Lacrosse World Cup. In 2018 Cummings joined the professional lacrosse team the New York Fight.

It is a sunny fall day at a neighborhood playing field. Girls run back and forth. Parents stand on the sideline cheering. There is a goal at each end of the field. The girls toss a small ball to each other. One player runs toward the goal. She flings the ball at the cage with her stick. It's a good shot, but the goalie catches it. Girls shout encouraging words to their teammates. Instead of giving high fives, they click their sticks together. This is a game of girls' lacrosse.

Taylor Cummings started playing lacrosse when she was around 6 years old. Taylor was named the best college athlete in the United States in 2016 and was chosen as a member of the U.S. Lacrosse Team. She was also one of the first members of the first professional women's lacrosse teams in the country.

Taylor helped the U.S. team win the lacrosse World Cup in 2017. She started her own business called Taylor Cummings Lacrosse, where young girls can sign up for lacrosse camps and classes. Taylor says lacrosse made her the person she is today, and she wants to help girls who love playing lacrosse reach their goals. Players like Taylor are helping girls' lacrosse become one of the country's most popular sports.

cage—the net players try to shoot the ball into in lacrosse

Lacrosse was invented by Native American tribes hundreds of years ago. They often used it as a way to settle problems. They also played to get stronger for battles. Games sometimes stretched over two or more days. Many people played at once. The game has changed a lot since then.

In the 1890s in Scotland, a group of girls played lacrosse at their school. It was the first recorded game played only by women. Their teacher, Louisa Lumsden, had seen a lacrosse game when she was visiting Canada. Once back in Scotland, she made up rules that were just for girls. Her students formed teams and played matches against each other. The winning team got a trophy.

Lacrosse sticks ranged in length from about 2 to 5 feet (0.6 to 1.5 meters) among different Native American tribes.

Lumsden's version of the game became popular in Great Britain. Later, one of her former students moved to the United States. Her name was Rosabelle Sinclair. She became a teacher at a girls' school called Bryn Mawr School. She started a lacrosse team for her students in 1926. By the 1940s, many girls' schools and colleges in the United States had lacrosse teams.

Native American lacrosse games often stretched over miles of terrain.

Girls' lacrosse today is not much different from those first games in Scotland. However, girls' lacrosse is different from boys' lacrosse in many ways. Girls wear less safety gear. Boys' teams have 10 players, and girls' teams have 12. Boys are allowed to body check. Girls are not allowed to body check. For both boys and girls, lacrosse is one of the fastest growing games in the United States.

check—to make contact with another player in order to get the ball away from the other player or slow the other player down

Lacrosse is not an Olympic sport—yet! However, the United States has had a women's lacrosse team since 1933. When the national team was first founded, it traveled around the world to play. Over time women in many other countries began playing lacrosse too. A group was formed to set up games for teams around the world. It is called the Federation of International Lacrosse (FIL). The FIL holds a lacrosse World Cup every four years. The U.S. team has won the lacrosse World Cup eight out of 10 times. FIL is trying to help women's lacrosse become an Olympic game. Soon young lacrosse players may have the chance to watch their favorite game at the Olympics.

1890

1926

1941

1982

2016

FACT

In some early Native American games of lacrosse, anywhere from 100 to 1,000 people played at one time.

Louisa Lumsden organizes the first game of girls' lacrosse at St. Leonards School in Scotland.

Rosabelle Sinclair establishes the first women's team in the United States at the Bryn Mawr School in Baltimore, Maryland.

The first women's game between two college teams is played with Sweet Briar College facing the College of William and Mary.

The first Women's Lacrosse World Cup is held, and the U.S. team wins the first of eight world championships.

Professional women's lacrosse begins in the U.S. when four teams form the United Women's Lacrosse League. Another league follows in 2018 with five teams. It is called the Women's Professional Lacrosse League.

The Ojibwa Loon

Some Native Americans used the sport of lacrosse to explain why birds go south in the winter. In one Ojibwa myth, summer was the only season. A type of bird called a loon wanted to play lacrosse all the time. He lost every game against a powerful hawk. The loon's punishment for losing was a cold winter wind. The loon and his friends had to fly south to get warm.

championship   a contest or tournament that decides which team is the best

9

GEAR OF THE GAME

All lacrosse players must have a stick. They use the stick to catch and pass a ball made of hard rubber. The stick that girls play with is between 35.4 and 43.3 inches (90 and 110 centimeters) long. It is called a crosse. The pocket on a girls' crosse must be made of mesh or string. The girls' lacrosse stick pocket is smaller than the boys' pocket. The smaller pocket makes **cradling** harder. Most people agree this makes the girls' game harder to play.

cradle—when a lacrosse player with the ball rocks it back and forth in her stick to control it

2

3

5

4

1. **Stick and Ball**
Sticks are made of wood, metal, fiberglass, or other man-made materials. Lacrosse balls are usually yellow, lime-green, or orange.

2. **Goggles**
Lacrosse goggles are like wire cages that protect the eyes and facial bones from impact. Some helmets have built-in goggles. Girls and women of all ages are required to wear goggles during games.

3. **Mouthguard**
A mouthguard is a piece of rubber that fits over the teeth. Mouthguards protect players' teeth and tongues during games.

4. **Gloves**
Lacrosse gloves are close-fitting. They are padded to protect the hands from cuts and blisters.

5. **Cleats**
Cleats are special sports shoes with small points on the bottom. Cleats keep players from slipping when they run.

Girls' lacrosse goggles are usually made with silicone padding and a protective cage or plastic lenses over the eyes.

Gear that Protects

Lacrosse is a fast-moving sport. There is always a chance of tripping, running into other players, or getting hit by a stick. Ankle and knee sprains are also common. Safety equipment can help players avoid getting hurt. Some safety equipment is required for girls' lacrosse. Girls have to wear goggles and a mouthguard. Girls can also wear gloves and special shoes called cleats.

Players can be hurt by a swinging stick, a collision with an opponent, or a stray ball. They even risk getting a concussion. Girls are not required to wear helmets, though. They can choose to wear them if they want. Headgear must cover the entire head, similar to a bike helmet. If players are wearing headgear, they must also have eye protection. Many girls' teams across the United States are adding a rule that requires players to wear helmets.

Girls' lacrosse goalkeepers must wear more safety equipment than field players. Goalies must wear a hard helmet. They also wear a face mask, a hard throat guard, padded gloves, a mouthpiece, and foam pads on their chest, pelvis, and legs. These guards keep goalies safe from swinging sticks and flying balls. The goalie's stick is different from a field player's crosse. It may be longer—35.4 inches to 53.1 inches (90 cm to 135 cm)—and has a much wider pocket. This helps the goalie stop the other team from scoring goals.

FACT

"Lacrosse" comes from the word crosse, which is the French word for the curved stick a bishop carries. Native American tribes like the Onondaga called the game *dehuntshigwa'es*, a word that meant "man hits ball."

The Evolution of the Ball

Some of the first lacrosse balls were pieces of burned wood. Some balls were made from animal hide. They were stuffed with fur, grass, or sand. The first goals were two trees that stood close together. Made from wood, the first sticks were similar to ones used today. They were curved with small pockets at the top. The pockets were small and made of animal skin. The sticks often had feathers tied to the tops.

concussion—an injury to the brain caused by a hard blow to the head

Attacker Rebecca Lane was chosen to play for the Australian national team in 2017. Her team placed fourth during the 2017 Women's Lacrosse World Cup.

Lacrosse has many rules, and breaking a rule can result in a penalty. Some rules are the same for boys and girls. Many are different, though. Girls have more players on the field than boys. There can be up to 12 players in a girls' game. Younger teams can have fewer players. On most teams there are attackers, midfielders, defenders, and a goalie.

Attackers are the players who score goals most often. Attackers work to get into scoring positions near the other team's goal. There can be up to three attackers on a team. Midfielders are the main ball carriers. Their job is to move the ball between attackers and defenders. There can be up to five midfielders on a team. Defenders protect their goalie. The three defenders try to stop the other team from taking shots. The goalie stays in front of or around the goal. She blocks shots to keep the other team from scoring.

penalty—a punishment for breaking the rules

The girls' field has a center circle. There is a line on each end of the field called a restraining line. Both goals have a small circle and a larger half circle around them.

Only seven players are allowed past the other team's restraining line at one time. If more than seven players cross the line, it is called offside. Only the goalie is allowed inside the goalie circle. If a player breaks one of these rules, the other team gets the ball.

Defensive players must allow attackers enough space to shoot safely. The shooting space is called the free space to goal. It is shaped like an ice-cream cone. The goal circle is the ice cream, and the tip of the cone is the attacker's crosse. If defensive players enter the cone while the attacker is trying to shoot the ball, a foul is called. Defenders can use their crosses in the cone without penalty. Attacking players are responsible for not shooting the ball at other players, or at the goalkeeper's body—this is called a dangerous shot.

Depending on her position, a girls' lacrosse player might run 2 to 5 miles (3 to 8 kilometers) in a single game.

Non-Contact Sport

Even though girls' lacrosse is action-packed, it is not a contact sport. Girls are not allowed to body check, or strike other players with their sticks. Stick checking is allowed once girls reach the level for players ages 11 to 12 (12U). Stick checking means that players can use their sticks to strike another player's stick. Checking is a way to get the ball from opponents. The player being checked must have the ball. A penalty is called if body checking is used. Penalties are also called if a stick touches another player's body or gets too close to her head. Player position is important in girls' lacrosse. A player cannot push into another player. This is called charging. A player must also carry her stick safely. If a player does not control her stick in a safe way, dangerous propelling is called. Players are given different colored cards for penalties.

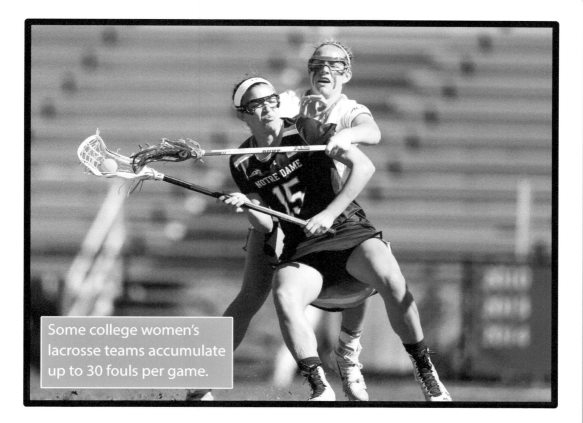

Some college women's lacrosse teams accumulate up to 30 fouls per game.

Cards in Girls' Lacrosse

Girls receive colored cards for penalties once they reach the under 10 (10U) level, or age nine. Green cards are given only to the team captain. They are given when a team keeps the game from starting on time. Yellow cards are for first-time penalties. Players who get a yellow card have a two-minute time-out. Red cards are given for repeat penalties. A red card means the player must sit out the rest of the game and is prohibited from participating in the team's next game. Red cards can be given to a player, coach, or any team personnel. A red card can also be given for unsportsmanlike behavior.

STRATEGIES TO SUCCEED

Midfielders Sammy Jo Tracy of the University of North Carolina Tar Heels and Allie Pavinelli of the University of Florida Gators challenged for a draw.

Once girls reach the 10U level, each lacrosse game begins with a draw in the middle of the field. Two opposing players stand across from each other. Their sticks are held sideways with the backs of the stick pockets touching each other. The sticks must be touching, and the bottom of the sticks must be level. The ball is placed between the stick pockets. When the referee blows the whistle, the girls can only move their sticks up and away. Sticks cannot be pushed out. The ball flies into the air. The team that gets the ball has "draw control." Starting once players reach 12U, there is also a draw after every score. A team who can win draws has an **advantage**.

In a draw, players are only allowed to move their heads until the sound of the whistle. They also cannot move their sticks toward the ground. If one of the players moves her hand or foot, the draw must be done again. If a player moves her stick toward the ground, the other team gets the ball.

advantage—a better chance of scoring

Scoring

Offense is the scoring part of the game. Speed is the number-one key to scoring. Attackers must beat the defense to the goal. Teamwork is also important. Girls must be aware of their teammates on the field. Talking to each other is important so everyone knows what to do.

To score, midfielders and attackers pass the ball quickly down the field. Many teams use triangle passing. This means the players pass the ball in a zigzag pattern until it reaches the goal. Speed and quick passes help a team keep the ball from their opponent.

Liz Bannantine scooped up ground balls 86 times while playing defense for Princeton University from 2013 to 2016.

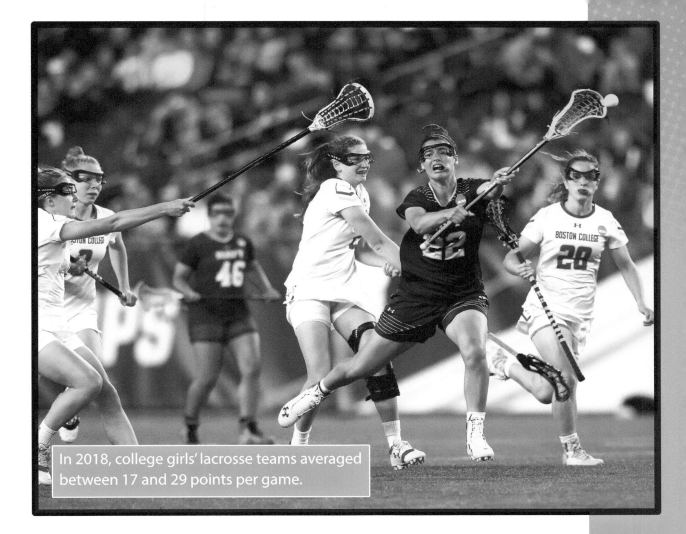

In 2018, college girls' lacrosse teams averaged between 17 and 29 points per game.

Once the ball reaches an attacker, she can take a shot. Shots can be taken close to the goal or on the run. Shooting on the run means a player does not stop to take a shot. A good shooter is good at faking. This means she makes the goalie think she is shooting one way, then shoots in a different direction.

Being able to prevent goals is just as important as being able to score. A strong defense allows the offense more opportunities to score.

Strategies for Scoring

Scoring is fun, but a winning team must have a strong defense. The defender's job is to keep the attacker from getting to the goal. Defenders can use their bodies to block an opponent's view of the goal. They can use their sticks to try to get the ball. Defenders can force opponents to pass the ball or go a different way. The two basic types of defense in girls' lacrosse are man-to-man and zone.

Man-to-man defense is the one teams use most. This means a player guards one opponent. She sticks to her mark like glue. She stays between her mark and the goal at all times. A player who is being guarded this way has a hard time shooting. Zone defense is when a player covers an area of the field. A player's zone changes as the ball moves around the field.

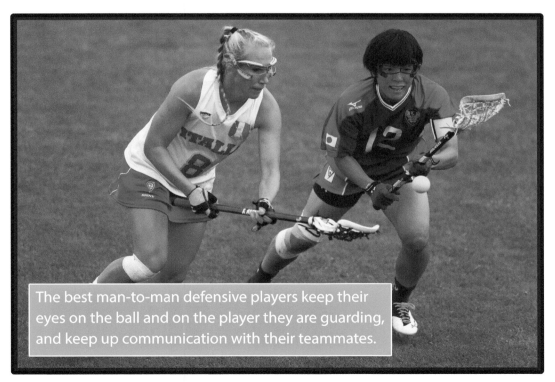

The best man-to-man defensive players keep their eyes on the ball and on the player they are guarding, and keep up communication with their teammates.

mark—a goal or target; in sports, the opponent that a player is guarding

READY TO PLAY?

Girls who want to learn the game of lacrosse are in luck! More people are playing lacrosse in the United States than ever before. High school girls' lacrosse teams compete in most states. Watching a game is a great way to learn about the rules and positions. College lacrosse games are shown on television. There are also many girls' lacrosse videos on the Internet. Classes and camps like the ones Taylor Cummings teaches can be found in many cities.

Before they join a team, new players should practice the basic skills. Girls can practice passing and shooting against a brick or concrete wall. New players should practice cradling and keeping the ball in the pocket. Getting a friend to practice with can be helpful. Starting a new sport can be easier with a buddy.

Running, exercising, and playing other sports help the body become more athletic. Drinking lots of water helps the body work properly. Eating well is important too. Being in great shape will make playing on a lacrosse team much easier.

The ideal wall for lacrosse practice is at least 10 feet (3 m) high. A long wall allows more space to move.

Joining a Team

There are youth US Lacrosse programs in 45 states. These programs have teams for girls of all ages. Being part of a team is a great way to learn the game. Trained coaches can teach players how to be safe on the field. New players can visit a local sporting goods store for gear. A salesperson can help players make sure they get the right items. They can also make sure gear like sticks and goggles are the right size.

Girls just starting out should be willing to learn every position. Knowing how to play everywhere on the field helps players understand the game better. New players should always play at the correct level for safety. The most important rule is to have fun! Learning a brand-new sport can be hard. However, playing on a team is a great way to learn and make new friends.

FACT

More than 160,000 girls play youth lacrosse in the United States each year. It is one of the fastest-growing youth sports in the country.

While girls' lacrosse teams might start training in late winter, games are played from spring through the end of the school year.

Glossary

advantage *(ad-VAN-tij)*—a better chance of scoring

cage *(KAYJ)*—the net players try to shoot the ball into in lacrosse

championship *(CHAM-pee-uhn-ship)*—a contest or tournament that decides which team is the best

check *(CHEK)*—to make contact with another player in order to get the ball away from the other player or slow the other player down

concussion *(kuhn-KUH-shuhn)*—an injury to the brain caused by a hard blow to the head

cradle *(KREYD-uhl)*—when a lacrosse player with the ball rocks it back and forth in her stick to control it

mark *(MARK)*—a goal or target; in sports, the opponent that a player is guarding

penalty *(PEN-uhl-tee)*—a punishment for breaking the rules

Read More

Maring, Therese Kauchak. *Sports & Fitness: How to Use Your Body and Mind to Play and Feel Your Best.* A Smart Girl's Guide. Middleton, WI: American Girl, 2018.

Rogers, Kate. *Girls Play Lacrosse.* New York: PowerKids Press, 2017.

Wiener, Gary. *Lacrosse: Science on the Field.* Science Behind Sports. New York: Lucent Press, 2018.

Internet Sites

College Women's Lacrosse
www.ncaa.com/sports/lacrosse-women/d1

Nutrition and Fitness Center
kidshealth.org/en/kids/center/fitness-nutrition-center.html

Women's Professional Lacrosse League
www.prowomenslax.com

Index

Bryn Mawr School, 7, 9

camps, 5, 26
Cummings, Taylor, 5, 26

equipment, 7, 10, 11, 12, 13, 28

Federation of International Lacrosse (FIL), 8

Lumsden, Louisa, 6, 7, 9

Native Americans, 6, 8, 9, 13

Olympics, 8

penalties, 15, 16, 18, 19

rules, 6, 12, 14, 15, 16, 18, 26, 28, 30

scoring, 13, 15, 21, 22, 24, 30

United Women's Lacrosse League, 9

Women's Professional Lacrosse League, 9
World Cup, 5, 8, 9